**CCSS** Genre Historical Fic

Essential Question
How do inventions and technology affect your life?

MW00615782

The Freedom Machine

by Paul Mason
illustrated by Dan Bridy

CHAPTER 1
The Latest Thing

I remember the first time I saw a car. I was walking home with my dad. We had big sacks of apples. Dad works for Mrs. Williams. He takes care of her large house and garden. I helped Dad pick apples, so Mrs. Williams told me to take some apples home. She is generous.

As Dad and I walked, we heard a weird noise. We turned around and saw a car driving in the middle of the road. The driver waved at us.

I said, "If we had a car, we wouldn't have to carry these heavy sacks."

My father shook his head. "Cars cost a lot of money. We can't afford a car. Anyway, I've got my bike." Then he pointed at my feet. "And your feet are made for walking," he joked.

"Dad!" I groaned.

"And the machines that move on rails, they are called trains," he teased.

cap

handlebar

I replied, "But, Dad, if we had a car, we could go anywhere we wanted. We could drive to the river and have a picnic."

I had another thought. "We could drive to the beach. I've never seen the ocean."

Dad wasn't convinced. He shook his head and said, "You think cars are wonderful, Alice, but I'm not sure that cars are so great."

STOP AND CHECK

Why does Alice want a car?

4

CHAPTER 2
Not a Toy

The following week, I went to Mrs. Williams's house with my dad. I could not believe my eyes. There was a shiny black car on the driveway.

"The car belongs to Mrs. Williams," Dad said. He was grinning. "It was delivered today."

Mrs. Williams was excited, too. "Mr. Dawson, you'll be the driver," she said to Dad.

<u>He was</u> worried. "I guess I'll have to learn how to drive," he said.

That night, Dad began reading the instruction book for the car. He practiced driving the car on Mrs. Williams's driveway every day. I wished I could learn to drive.

Language Detective	<u>He was</u> shows pronoun-verb agreement. What other pronouns agree with the verb *was?*

One afternoon, Dad came home covered in dust. The twins and I laughed at him.

My mom asked, "How did you get so dusty and dirty?"

He replied, "I drove Mrs. Williams to see her friend in Brownsville. We drove 20 miles on a dry and dusty road. The roads are made for horses and carts, not cars."

Dad continued, "Mrs. Williams was so bothered. The wind almost blew her hat away. I prefer a horse and carriage to a car."

Language Detective	I is the pronoun in the sentence. What verb agrees with I?

Mrs. Williams

dust

headlight

The next day, I helped my dad clean Mrs. Williams's car. The car was covered in dust.

We washed, wiped, polished, and brushed the car inside and out. When we had finished, the paintwork and brass headlights gleamed.

I put my hands on the steering wheel and pretended to drive. I squirmed and wriggled on the leather seat.

"Can you show me how to start the engine? Can we go for a ride?" I pleaded.

Dad replied, "No, Alice. The car isn't a toy. And I can't waste gas and oil."

"Can we go for a ride one day?" I asked, but Dad didn't reply.

STOP AND CHECK

How did Alice's father get so dusty?

CHAPTER 3
Steam and an Offer

A few days later, I got to ride in the car! My dad and I were picking apples when Mrs. Williams decided to visit her nephew. She asked my dad, "Can you please drive me to the train station? I want to catch the one o'clock train."

Dad took out his pocket watch. "We should leave now to make sure we get to the station on time," he replied.

Mrs. Williams was surprised. "We have plenty of time. That car can travel at 35 miles per hour," she said.

Dad explained, "That's possible on a smooth road, but the road to the train station wasn't made for cars."

Mrs. Williams replied, "If you say so, Mr. Dawson." She winked at me. "I guess we'll take Alice, too. I know how much she likes cars."

I sat in the front next to my dad. I watched his hands gripping the wheel and listened to the engine. I felt the wind on my face. I couldn't believe how fast we were going.

Suddenly we heard a hissing sound. Steam came out of the engine. Dad stopped the car on the side of the road. He opened the hood and tinkered with the engine. "The car has overheated. We need to put water in the radiator," he said.

steam

hood

"There's no water around here," Mrs. Williams said. She had a worried frown on her face. "What will we do? I don't want to miss the train."

Dad was worried, too. "You wouldn't have this trouble with a horse," he said quietly.

Mrs. Williams reached inside her bag and removed a bottle and a cup. She unscrewed the lid of the bottle and was pouring a drink.

"Mrs. Williams, is that water?" I asked.

"Why, yes," Mrs. Williams replied. Then it hit her. "Good thinking, Alice!" she said. She got out of the car and handed the bottle to Dad.

"We need to wait for the radiator to cool before I put the water in it," Dad said.

We sat and waited. Finally, my dad said, "I hope that this works, Mrs. Williams." He poured the water into the radiator.

> **In Other Words** she realized. En español, *it hit her* quiere decir *se dió cuenta*.

Dad turned the crank, and the engine started. He drove as fast as he dared. The car bumped and rattled along the rough road.

When we arrived at the station, we saw the train arriving at the platform. Dad grabbed Mrs. Williams's suitcase and gave it to the porter on the train.

Mrs. Williams said, "Thank you, Mr. Dawson. You were right to allow extra time. And if it weren't for Alice's quick thinking, I'd have missed the train. I would like to thank you. Why don't you use the car for a day."

I was so excited that I almost fell over. Even dad whistled as we drove back into town.

STOP AND CHECK

What happened on the way to the train station?

train

platform

suitcase

11

CHAPTER 4
To the Sea

That night, Dad told the family about Mrs. Williams's offer. "You know, I'm starting <u>to get used to</u> this new technology. I think we'll all enjoy a day at the beach," he said, smiling.

On Saturday, Mom directed me while we made a picnic lunch. Then Dad crammed the picnic basket under the car seat. Mom and Baby John sat in the front of the car. The twins and I squeezed into the backseat.

I grinned at the twins. I told them, "You're going to love this."

Dad turned the crank, and the engine started. He climbed into the driver's seat, and we were off.

After we left the town, Dad drove faster. The car shuddered and rattled on the uneven roads, but we were excited.

> **In Other Words** become familiar with. En español, *to get used to* quiere decir *acostombrarse.*

The beach was even better than we imagined. The ocean sparkled, the sun shone, and the sand was almost white.

Mom and Baby John played by the water. Dad watched me and the twins play in the waves.

Then the twins and I explored the rock pools, where we scouted for treasures. We found seaweed, shells, starfish, and tiny fish.

We had a great day at the beach. It was all because of the car, the freedom machine.

Eventually, it was time to go home, so we packed up and got into the car. Baby John slept next to Mom in the backseat. I sat in the front seat beside Dad.

On the way home, we passed some people picking apples, and they waved at us.

"I guess they think this is our car," Dad said.

"I wish it was ours," I sighed.

My dad said, "You might be right about cars, Alice. Cars really can take you places!"

STOP AND CHECK

What did Alice's family do at the beach?

apple tree

wave

basket

Respond to Reading

Summarize

Use important details to summarize *The Freedom Machine*. Your graphic organizer may help you.

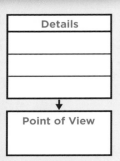

Details

↓

Point of View

Text Evidence

1. What features in *The Freedom Machine* indicate that the story is historical fiction? GENRE

2. Describe the point of view from which the story is told. Give examples from the text. **POINT OF VIEW**

3. Find a synonym for *crammed* on page 12. **SYNONYMS**

4. Write about how the story would be different if it were told by a third-person narrator. **WRITE ABOUT READING**

Compare Texts
Read about the effect the interstate highway system had on people in the United States.

The Interstate Highway System

In the early twentieth century, cars became more common in the United States. At that time, most roads were not paved. It took a long time to drive on unpaved roads, and the ride was bumpy and uncomfortable.

A few decades later, in the 1950s, people began to think about building a highway system.

Poor roads made travel difficult for cars. This photograph from 1909 shows a car stuck in the mud.

horse

unpaved road

17

President Dwight D. Eisenhower realized that highways were useful. People could travel, and goods could move easily across the country.

In 1956, Eisenhower persuaded Congress to pass the Federal-Aid Highway Act. More than 40,000 miles (64,373 kilometers) of highways were built throughout the United States. The government paid the cost of building most of the interstate highway system.

All highways had at least two lanes in each direction.

How Interstate Highways Are Numbered

Every interstate highway has a number. Major routes have one- or two-digit numbers. Interstate highways with odd numbers run north and south. Interstate highways with even numbers run east and west.

Three-digit numbers are used for highways around a city and for routes that join different interstate highways.

In some places, it was an engineering challenge to build highways. Engineers had to blast through large hills to build highways.

When the new highway system was built, people could travel long distances quickly. Goods could be transported across the country directly in trucks.

The interstate highway system helped make people's lives easier. The highway system also changed communities because people could live farther from the centers of towns and cities.

Bridges were built so the highway could run above the roads.

Make Connections

How did interstate highways affect people's lives?
ESSENTIAL QUESTION

How would cars and highways change the lives of ordinary people like Alice? **TEXT TO TEXT**

Focus on Genre

Historical Fiction tells a story that is set in the past. It often gives information about a real event or is based on real facts. Historical fiction gives the reader an understanding of life in the past.

Read and Find A story that is set in the past usually includes dates, events, or other objects that help show the reader when the story is set. Find details from the story that tell you *The Freedom Machine* is set in the past. For example, the dirt roads.

Your Turn

Work with a partner. Plan a road trip for Alice's family. For example, Alice's family might attend a fair in a nearby town.

Write sentences to describe the trip. Use details from the story to help you. Remember that the story takes place in the past, so include details from the past, such as the clothes the characters wear.